85p

COOKING WITH YOGURT

IRFAN ORGA

Cooking with Yogurt

ANDRE DEUTSCH

FIRST PUBLISHED 1956 BY
ANDRE DEUTSCH LIMITED
105 GREAT RUSSELL STREET LONDON WC1
SECOND IMPRESSION FEBRUARY 1975
ALL RIGHTS RESERVED

PRINTED AND BOUND IN GREAT BRITAIN BY
REDWOOD BURN LIMITED
TROWBRIDGE AND ESHER

ISBN 0 233 96653 6

CONTENTS

AUTHOR'S NOTE

✦✦✦✦✦✦✦✦✦✦✦✦✦✦✦✦✦✦✦✦✦✦✦✦✦✦✦

IN WRITING this book it has been my aim to extend the average person's knowledge as to the uses of yoğurt.

Yoğurt (pronounced yort) has been used by the Turks and Bulgars for so many centuries that its origin is quite lost in the mists of time. It has been introduced into Europe and America in very recent years and the majority of people who eat it, because they have been told it is good for them, know remarkably little about it. It is, of course, a harmless microbe which acts on fresh milk and transforms it into yoğurt and is known in the medical world as the *Bacillus Bulgaris*. This denotes its origin. In the Balkans sheep's milk is regarded as the best milk from which to make yoğurt but as sheep's milk is rather indigestible, invalids and convalescents are fed on the yoğurt made from cow's milk. In fact, yoğurt is such an important aid to good health that every hospital in Turkey serves it to patients as a matter of course. Twenty-three million Turks eat it daily (but *never* with sugar unless it is part of a dessert) and it is only produced on a commercial basis in the cities, for no Turkish housewife would dream of buying something that can be made three or four times cheaper at home and without trouble. In this book I have given the method for producing thick, sweet, fresh yoğurt in the home. It is the method which has been used successfully in my family for five generations.

Now for a few words as to the therapeutic qualities of yoğurt. As a medicine it might well be called a miracle worker and I have seen it act successfully on a dog which had been poisoned. It is so powerful that it fights and destroys the harmful germs that breed in the intestines – the cause of many of our diseases. Daily use of yoğurt ensures regular habits, the blood is purified and skin diseases cleared in a very short time. It is remarkably efficient in all intestinal troubles. For feverish conditions it can be given safely *when no other food is allowed;* it induces sleep and calms the nerves and thus has a remarkable effect on hysterical subjects. In Turkey pregnant women are recommended to eat yoğurt, or drink it as ayran (recipe given in this book) in preference to fresh milk, and nursing mothers include yoğurt in their diet as a matter of course.

Medical observations have proved that the yoğurt bacillus remains alive even *after the passage through the intestines* whilst the bacillus of other milk products cannot survive this. In the east of Turkey, where the people are very strong, it is considered that yoğurt, eaten with crushed garlic, is a certain preventative for tuberculosis. The peasants attribute their longevity and resistance to disease to yoğurt and outside every hut in summer – when the temperature is in the hundreds – you will see a large vessel covered by an old sack where the family yoğurt is setting. Yoğurt is a natural food and because the bacillus is not fussy about its breeding conditions it only needs the simplest equipment. The most important point is that the bacillus should be fresh, which means more sweet than sour, for sour bacillus makes sour yoğurt – although this will correct itself in time as I have shown in the following pages.

A good deal of nonsense has been talked about chilling, so let me say as emphatically as possible that chilling on ice is not recommended. Keep the yoğurt in a cool, even cold, larder, by all means, but do not refrigerate.

The following recipes are designed to give you the maximum pleasure from yoğurt. To see a bottle of yoğurt, a few days old more than likely and acid as vinegar, served with fruit pulp and sugar which has dissolved into a watery mass, is a revolting sight and unlikely to appeal even to the healthiest appetite. To one brought up on fresh, sweet yoğurt it is nothing less than tragedy to see how Europeans accept the thinness and sourness of yoğurt as inevitable. Yoğurt should be capable of being cut with a spoon and should never be of near-pourable consistency. It should be thick and smooth, without a trace of lumpiness, and should be the colour of cream. Powdered, tinned, skimmed or condensed milk will *not* make the yoğurt of the Balkans, but cream, because of the high content of butter-fat, is the ideal medium. In Turkey on very special feast days the yoğurt is made with fresh cream but this is far too extravagant for the ordinary household. Cow's milk is excellent and from now on I hope you will start making your own yoğurt and find enjoyment in testing the following recipes – as well as perhaps enjoying more perfect health than you have known before.

Istanbul, surely the most cosmopolitan city in the world, makes more use of yoğurt than any other city in Turkey. The dishes of many nations are represented in every menu, but French influence – being the strongest – has given us the most luxurious. All the recipes in this book have been used in my own family or have been collected through the years from Turkish friends, and whilst there are yoğurt recipes in most Turkish cookery books this is, I believe, the first book of yoğurt recipes ever to appear in the English language. I am indebted to many Turkish cooks and cookery writers for the basis of some of my recipes but it is to Madame Fahriye Nedim that I am most indebted. Her little book *Yemek, Tatli ve Pastalar* is a very treasured possession in my family. Her ideas are simple and direct, her housewifely wisdom inexhaustible (no yoğurt ever fails for her, for she's up to all its tricks) and she recognises the value of primitive methods for primitive foods. For yoğurt, dress it up as you may, is a primitive food – one of nature's blessings to mankind.

Publisher's note to the second impression of *Cooking with Yogurt*.
Since this book was first published it has become easy to buy simple and efficient yogurt-making equipment, which many people may prefer to home-made equipment. One such machine is the Yogomagic, which is widely available (if you cannot find a supplier, enquire of Parlane Associates, 11 - 21A Queen Caroline Street, London w6).

APPROXIMATE MEASUREMENTS

Almonds (shelled)	1 lb	approximately	3½	cups
Bananas (sliced)	1 lb	"	2½	"
Butter	1 lb	"	2	"
Cheese (grated)	1 lb	"	4	"
Cheese (soft white)	1 lb	"	2	"
Cream (heavy)	1 pint	"	2	"
Cream (whipped)	1 pint	"	4	"
Dates (whole)	1 lb	"	2¼	"
Dates (stoned)	1 lb	"	2	"
Dates (cut up)	1 lb	"	1¾	"
Figs (cut up)	1 lb	"	2¾	"
Flour (sifted)	1 lb	"	4	"
Prunes (cooked, stoned)	1 lb	"	4	"
Prunes (cooked, cut up)	1 lb	"	3	"
Raisins (cut up)	1 lb	"	2¾	"
Rice	1 lb	"	2¼	"
Sugar (brown)	1 lb	"	2	"
Sugar (caster)	1 lb	"	2¼	"
Sugar (icing, sifted)	1 lb	"	3¼	"
Walnuts (shelled)	1 lb	"	4	"

IMPORTANT NOTE

All measurements in this book are calculated according to
the theory that 250 ccs equal 1 cup – whether for dry or
liquid ingredients. The *Pyrex* standard measuring cup
shows the 250 ccs mark.

COOKING WITH YOGURT

YOGURT MAKES YOGURT

◊◊◊◊◊◊◊◊◊◊◊◊◊◊◊◊◊◊◊◊◊◊◊◊◊◊◊

IT MIGHT be as well to explain from the outset that to obtain the bacillus required to transform your milk into yoğurt you will first have to buy a small bottle of ordinary yoğurt to start you off. From this you will have to reserve one-half of a teaspoon of the yoğurt and this is your fermenting agent or bacillus. A good many people are confused by the words 'bacillus' or 'yoğurt' but the truth is that yoğurt is its own bacillus and goes on breeding for ever. So that having bought your first yoğurt from outside and reserved the necessary one-half teaspoon you will not need to do so again. Your own daily yoğurt will supply the bacillus needed.

EQUIPMENT NEEDED TO MAKE YOĞURT AT HOME

1 *8-inch cake tin with cover*
1 *yard cotton twill*
A good handful of feathers (these can be taken from a spare pillow and the difference will never be noticed)
4 *glass bottles (4 fluid oz) or* 3 *glass bottles (5 fluid oz)*
A cork mat big enough to cover the tops of the yoğurt bottles when they are standing in the tin
1 *table napkin*

The cake tin has to be lined with padding. For this use the cotton twill and feathers, making a round cushion for the bottom of the tin, another to go under the lid, and a long-shaped one with which to line the sides.

The top and bottom cushions need not be stuffed very full, just enough to make a firm base for the bottles to stand on and to allow the lid to be easily manipulated. The side lining, however, should be more tightly packed. Make certain that the round cushions and the side lining fit snugly against each other.

INGREDIENTS

1 *pint fresh milk*   ½ *teaspoon yoğurt*

Put the milk in a saucepan and bring to boil. Let the froth rise to the top and boil for one minute. Remove from heat, cool 3 to 4 minutes, stirring frequently to prevent a skin forming and to help the cooling process. Pour into the bottles, which should be resting on the napkin in their 'nest' and cool to 106°/109°. If you have no thermometer there is no need to panic – just test with your little finger and the correct degree will have been reached approximately when your finger can comfortably resist the heat. Take the ½ teaspoon of yoğurt and mix with 3 teaspoons of warm milk from the bottles. Divide this bacillus amongst the remaining milk in the bottles and stir well. Place the cork mat in position, draw up the four edges of the napkin to cover, put the top pillow in place and cover the whole with the lid of the cake tin. Leave to set for 8 hours or preferably overnight. Cool uncovered in the 'nest' two or three hours before serving.

Here are a few points to remember to ensure that your yoğurt-making will be a success:

Once the yoğurt is made, handle the tin as little as possible until set.

Room temperature of not less than 65° is essential. A kitchen above that temperature is all to the good.

Do not try to use the yoğurt until the minimum setting time (8 hours) has been reached or it will be little heavier than the consistency of thick cream. To obtain a thicker yoğurt in less time would mean the expenditure of more bacillus which is not recommended. Yoğurt made with more bacillus will not be as creamy because the bacillus has no room to expand and the finished product will be *a mass of tiny globules*. It can never achieve the same result as the yoğurt made with the smaller amount of bacillus.

Make your yoğurt daily – always remembering to reserve a little from the previous day. *The bacillus lives indefinitely*. At least a week, perhaps two, will elapse before your home-made product begins to get sweeter, but it will not sour again unless you use sour (old) bacillus.

In the case of failure one of the following is likely to have happened:

(*a*) the milk was too hot or too cool when the bacillus was inserted, or

(*b*) the 'nest' was insufficiently feathered and so could not retain the heat.

If you are too faint-hearted to continue by the finger-testing method, now is the time to rush out and buy a thermometer. It is also a good plan to reserve at least one teaspoon of the previous day's yoğurt so that mistakes may be remedied. But the failed yoğurt *can* be made to set, so there is no need to throw away the milk. Put the bottles in a saucepan of *warm* water (let the water cover two-thirds of the spoiled bottles of yoğurt) and leave for a few hours, renewing the water as it cools below blood heat.

In yoğurt-making, like everything else, practice makes perfect and by the end of the first week you will be an old hand at it. Do keep in mind that from the time the milk has been put into the bottles the correct degree of heat will be reached in *a minute or two*.

It is possible to buy special equipment for making yoğurt, but this expenditure is not necessary. You may, of course, use the yoğurt sold in shops if you wish – it is perfectly wholesome and many people find its flavour agreeable – but it bears very little resemblance to yoğurt made at home and its effect in the following recipes will not be the same.

SOUPS

❖❖❖❖❖❖❖❖❖❖❖❖❖❖❖❖❖❖❖❖❖❖❖

ADANA SOUP

4 cups beef stock
2 cups self-raising flour
4 tablespoons water
1 egg
1 egg yolk
½ lb lean minced beef

3 onions (finely chopped)
¼ cup soft butter
1 teaspoon pepper
½ tablespoon garlic salt
4 tablespoons minced
   parsley

GARNISHING

2 tablespoons butter
2 cups fresh yoğurt

1 teaspoon fresh thyme (chopped)
2 teaspoons fresh mint (chopped)

Melt butter in stewpan, add onions and sauté until transparent. Add minced beef. Cook five minutes. Add parsley, salt and pepper and cook a further 15 minutes. Remove from heat and cool. Sift the flour in a mixing bowl. Make a well and add the egg yolk, whole egg and water. Mix together and knead into a stiff dough. Cover with a damp cloth and leave to rest for one hour.

Roll out very thinly on floured board. Put the meat mixture in teaspoonsful one inch in from the top edge of the pastry and half-inch apart from each other. Fold top edge over, seal with water and cut into tiny fancy shapes. Repeat with the rest of the pastry and meat mixture. Bring the stock to boiling point, drop in the pastries and boil gently for about 15 minutes.

Whisk the yoğurt with 2 teaspoons water and stir into the soup. Do not boil again. Serve with garnishing of melted butter, thyme and mint.

BORTSCH SOUP

4 *cups bouillon*
1 *small onion*
1 *cup white cabbage*
1 *cup red cabbage*
1 *tablespoon tomato purée*
4 *raw beets*
1 *clove crushed garlic*
1 *green pepper*
1 *large potato*

½ *tablespoon fresh dill*
  (*finely chopped*)
2 *tablespoons lemon juice*
½ *cup yoğurt*
1 *tablespoon parsley*
  (*minced*)
½ *teaspoon pepper*
Salt to taste

Put the lemon juice in a bowl. Skin the beetroot, grate, extract the juice from half and add to the lemon juice.

Put the stock in a saucepan and bring to boil. Add garlic, tomato purée and dill. Grate vegetables and add to stock, including the beets. Cook 10–15 minutes and season to taste. Add the lemon and beet juice and stir well.

Whisk the yoğurt and combine with parsley. Drop as a garnish on the soup which should be served very hot.

CHICKEN SOUP WITH YOGURT

1 *broiler (about 3 lb)*	3 *egg yolks*
6 *cups water*	3 *whole eggs*
1 *carrot*	1 *teaspoon fennel*
1 *onion*	1 *teaspoon sweet marjoram*
1 *stalk of celery*	*Salt and pepper*
1 *cup yoğurt*	

Put broiler into large stewpan. Add the water and bring to boil slowly, removing the scum as it rises. Add vegetables and cook until chicken is tender (2½–3 hours). Remove chicken from stock and cut in thin strips, Julienne fashion. Strain stock and return to stewpan. Add pieces of chicken.

Whisk yoğurt in a bowl with the egg yolks, add the whole eggs and whisk well. Thin with a little of the stock and season. Add yoğurt mixture to stewpan and stir well but do not allow to boil. Serve hot, garnished with a little fennel and marjoram.

LOBSTER SOUP

4 *cups court bouillon (fish*
   stock)
½ *cup yoğurt*
1 *sliver of garlic*
1 *tablespoon butter*
3 *cups skinned, chopped*
   tomatoes
1 *medium-sized lobster (cooked)*

1 *tablespoon water*
½ *cup* Graves
2 *onions*
½ *teaspoon fresh thyme*
½ *teaspoon fresh fennel*
Pinch of nutmeg
Salt and pepper

Chop the onions and sauté in butter until transparent. Add tomatoes, garlic, herbs and seasoning. Cover and simmer for 25 minutes. Add the wine and boil for 3 minutes. Put in half the lobster, cut in pieces, and the court bouillon. Cook for 15 minutes and remove from heat. Put through a sieve, return to pan and add the rest of the lobster. Stir in the yoğurt, previously whisked with 1 tablespoon water until smooth. Heat and serve immediately.

SHRIMP SOUP (ICED)

1 ½ *cups cooked shrimps*
4 *cups court bouillon*
½ *cup yoğurt*
1 *egg yolk*
½ *cup cream*
¼ *cup white wine*
3 *tablespoons bread crumbs*

1 *tablespoon lemon rind*
   (grated)
1 *teaspoon chopped chives*
1 *teaspoon minced parsley*
½ *small cucumber*
Nutmeg
Salt and pepper

Pound half the shelled shrimps in a mortar. Put in a stewpan and add the wine and a pinch of nutmeg. Add breadcrumbs, lemon rind and the court bouillon, stirring all the time. Boil for 5–7 minutes. Sieve and return to stewpan. Beat the egg yolk and cream together and add to mixture. Heat but do not boil. Remove from heat and cool. Add half small cucumber, diced, the chives and parsley. Garnish with the rest of the shrimps. Ice and serve with fresh yoğurt.

SOUPE A LA TARTAR

8 *cups duck stock*
1 *tablespoon red currant jelly*
1 *cup red wine*
¼ *cup butter*
3 *shallots*
1 *lb minced duck meat*

2 *teaspoons grated lemon peel*
2 *cups yoğurt*
1 *egg*
1 *egg yolk*
2 *teaspoons finely chopped lemon verbena*
Salt and pepper

Bring stock to boil. Add the red currant jelly and wine, stir well and boil until slightly reduced (about five minutes). Melt butter in a pan. Put in shallots and sauté for three minutes. Add minced duck and lemon rind and cook for another three minutes. Stir this mixture into stock and season.

Whisk the yoğurt, the whole egg and the egg yolk and pour into stewpan, stirring all the time. Heat thoroughly but do not allow to boil. Garnish with lemon verbena.

SPINACH SOUP

4 *cups veal stock*
½ *lb spinach* (*cooked*)
2 *carrots*
3 *tablespoons butter*
4 *tablespoons flour*
1 *onion* (*chopped*)
4 *egg yolks*

2 *teaspoons dill*
1 *cup yoğurt*
½ *cup dry cider*
1 *stalk celery*
½ *clove crushed garlic*
2 *teaspoons minced parsley*
Salt and pepper

Bring the stock to boil in large stewpan. Add carrots and celery and cook until tender. Remove vegetables from stock and cut into strips, Julienne fashion. Keep hot.

Melt the butter and sauté onion until transparent. Add crushed garlic and flour, cook for 2 minutes and combine half cup stock to this by degrees, stirring all the time. Return to large stewpan and add spinach, parsley, dill, cooked vegetables and cider. Season and bring to boil.

Whisk yoğurt and egg yolks and add to stewpan. Do not allow to boil again. Serve hot.

◊○◊○◊○◊○◊○◊○◊○◊○◊○◊○◊○◊○◊○◊○◊○◊○

SERBIAN COD

1 *lb fillets*	2 *tablespoons Graves*
1 *lb small potatoes*	1 *teaspoon sifted flour*
1 *large onion*	1 *teaspoon paprika*
3 *tablespoons butter*	1 *cup yoğurt*
4 *medium tomatoes* (*sliced*)	*Salt and pepper*

Soak the fillets in salt water for ½ hour.

Peel and slice the potatoes and onion and put in a fire-proof dish. Dot with the butter. Slice the tomatoes and add to dish. Add the wine and sprinkle with salt and pepper. Cover and put into slow medium oven (325°) until the potatoes are half cooked – about 25 minutes.

Dry the fish and add to the vegetables. Mix flour and paprika and sprinkle over. Pour on the yoğurt and cook for 35–40 minutes or until fish is cooked.

HADDOCK A LA CREME

1 lb haddock
1 bay leaf
3 tablespoons grated cheese
1 onion, chopped

Enough yoğurt to cover
A little fried parsley
Salt and pepper

Clean and wash the haddock, cut into serving pieces and arrange in a buttered baking dish.

Heat the yoğurt (beaten previously with 1 tablespoon fish stock or water). Put in the bay leaf and onion, bring almost to boiling point. Remove from heat and strain. Pour this over the fish, bake at 350° for 1 hour. Sprinkle a little grated cheese over the whole and brown under a fierce grill until a gratin forms. Serve hot, garnished with fried parsley.

CREAMED RED MULLET

6 small red mullet
2 shallots (finely chopped)
1 cup red Burgundy
6 tomatoes (skinned)

2 tablespoons soft butter
½ cup yoğurt
Salt and pepper
Sorrel leaves

Wash and clean the fish. Dry and place in a buttered glass baking dish and sprinkle with the shallots. Pour over the wine and add the tomatoes, chopped. Cover and bake in 400° oven for about 25 minutes or until fish is cooked. Remove from oven, take out the fish and keep hot.

In a stewpan reduce the liquor by two-thirds and combine the butter. Season. Add well-beaten yoğurt and pour the whole over the fish. Garnish with a few sorrel leaves and serve at once.

SALMON A LA TURQUE

1 ½ cups salmon stock	¼ cup red wine
3 lb salmon	1 grated carrot
3 cups cooked spinach (chopped)	1 onion
	1 stalk of celery
½ cup grated Parmesan	1 bay leaf
4 tablespoons sifted flour	3 cloves
1 cup thick yoğurt	5 peppercorns
Dash of nutmeg	1 clove garlic
Salt	1 teaspoon thyme

Clean and scale the salmon and place in a deep kettle with enough *boiling* water to cover. Add the wine, carrot, onion, celery, bay leaf, cloves, peppercorns, garlic and thyme. Simmer gently until fish is easily separated from bone, but avoid overcooking as this will make the salmon dry. Remove fish from stock, drain and keep hot. Reduce stock by fierce, uncovered boiling to 1½ cups. Strain. Thicken the stock with flour and cook 10–12 minutes, stirring continuously to prevent lumps. Add the beaten yoğurt and nutmeg and stir well. Season.

Arrange the salmon on a bed of spinach, cover with the yoğurt sauce, sprinkle with Parmesan and put in a very hot oven (475°) until the cheese is delicately browned – about 3 minutes. Serve immediately.

BLUE TROUT WITH WHITE WINE

4 *trout*
1 *cup dry Sauterne*
1 *cup water*
1 *onion, quartered*
1 *bay leaf*
4 *sprigs chopped parsley*

½ *tablespoon basil*
½ *tablespoon tarragon*
1 *stalk celery*
¼ *cup yoğurt*
¼ *cup Hollandaise sauce*
Salt and pepper

Put the wine, water, onion, bay leaf, parsley, basil, tarragon, celery and seasoning into a large kettle. Bring to the boil and simmer for 1½ hours. Strain and keep hot.

Clean and empty the trout, put in cold water for a few minutes then drain and dry carefully. Add to the strained stock, bring to boil slowly and cook about 10 or 12 minutes. Serve with a combination of well-beaten yoğurt mixed with an equal quantity of Hollandaise sauce.

TROUT MENDERES

6 *fresh trout*
3 *tablespoons butter (soft)*
Dash of sweet marjoram

½ *cup thick yoğurt*
½ *cup heavy cream*
Salt and pepper

Clean fish and dry well. Place in a buttered glass baking dish, add the butter and the marjoram. Pour the beaten yoğurt and cream over and bake at 350° for 30 minutes or until fish is cooked. Serve at once.

BAKED TURBOT

1 *lb turbot*	2 *tablespoons white wine*
1 *cup yoğurt*	1 *tablespoon lemon juice*
1 *egg yolk*	2 *tablespoons minced*
1 *blade of mace*	*parsley*
¾ *cup buttered crumbs*	*Salt and pepper*

Arrange the cleaned fish in a buttered baking dish. Cover with beaten yoğurt, lemon juice, wine, mace and beaten egg yolk. Add the seasoning. Cover with the buttered crumbs and bake at 375° for 45–50 minutes. Serve hot, garnished with minced parsley.

◈◈◈◈◈◈◈◈◈◈◈◈◈◈◈◈◈◈◈◈◈◈◈◈◈◈◈◈

STUFFED RIBS OF BEEF WITH
RED CABBAGE

2 lb beef ribs
½ teaspoon carraway seeds
½ teaspoon sage
1 tablespoon dry sherry
¼ cup yoğurt
½ cup toasted crumbs

½ teaspoon basil
2 tablespoons finely minced onion
Garlic salt
Pepper

Season the ribs with a little garlic salt, add pepper and rub with melted butter. Beat the yoğurt and mix with the crumbs, carraway seeds, sherry, herbs and onions. If this mixture seems too dry add 1 tablespoon single cream.

Spread this over the seasoned ribs, roll up and tie securely with string to prevent the stuffing coming out. Put in a roasting dish and bake at 325° for 2¼ hours. Remove string before serving.

Arrange cooked, chopped red cabbage on a hot serving plate and sprinkle with wine vinegar. Place the stuffed ribs on this and spoon another cup of thick, unbeaten yoğurt over the ribs. Serve at once.

BOEUF ABDULLAH

1 *lb minced beef*	1 *cup yoğurt*
2 *thick slices day-old bread*	*White bread crumbs*
(crusts removed), soaked	*Salt and pepper*
in milk	1 *egg*
1 *medium onion (chopped)*	¾ *cup chopped mushrooms*
½ *cup butter*	

Fry onion in some of the butter until transparent. Remove from heat and cool a little. Mix well together the meat, onion, egg, bread and seasoning. Shape into small balls, flatten slightly, roll in toasted white bread crumbs and brown slowly in butter. Add the yoğurt and mushrooms and simmer for 30 minutes. Serve hot.

BOEUF MARDI

1 *lb finely minced beef*
2 *tablespoons wine vinegar*
1½ *cups yoğurt*
1 *cup sliced tomatoes*
4 *tablespoons butter*

3 *tablespoons flour*
1 *cup sliced mushrooms*
Celery salt
Paprika

Melt the butter in a deep stewpan and sauté the mushrooms for 5 minutes. Remove the mushrooms and keep hot. Put in the minced beef and cook until browned, add vinegar and flour and stir very well. Add tomatoes. Beat the yoğurt until smooth and combine with meat mixture. Season and add the mushrooms. Cook for another 5 minutes, stirring all the time. Pour into a baking dish, cover and cook at 300° for 1–1¼ hours. Serve hot with finely shredded horseradish worked into a little soft butter.

BOEUF A LA STROGONOFF

1 *lb fillet of beef*
4 *tablespoons butter*
1 *large onion (chopped finely)*
½ *tablespoon tomato purée*

1 *teaspoon mustard (dry)*
1 *cup yoğurt*
1 *tablespoon flour*
½ *teaspoon pepper*
Salt to taste

Melt the butter in a stewpan and fry onion lightly. Cut the meat in strips half an inch wide and one inch long, and add to the onions. Fry for about 5 minutes until meat begins to brown. Add the flour and stir well. Add tomato purée, mustard, pepper and salt and cook a further 4 or 5 minutes. Add the yoğurt and bring to boil gently. Remove from heat immediately and serve at once.

CHICKEN CONTINENTALE

6 tablespoons chicken fat
1½ cups rich chicken stock
½ cup yoğurt
¼ cup good sherry
1 cup cooked green peas
¼ cup green pepper, thinly
   sliced
6 tablespoons flour
½ cup single cream

1 cup cooked chicken,
   cut in pieces
1 cup sliced mushrooms
¼ cup pimento, thinly
   sliced
4 tablespoons butter
Dash of cayenne
Garlic salt

Sauté the mushrooms in a pan until slightly brown. Melt the chicken fat in a separate pan, blend in flour and seasoning and cook over a low heat until bubbling. Remove from heat and add stock and cream. Stir well. Beat the yoğurt and blend in gradually. Bring to boiling point, stirring all the time, and boil for 1 minute. Add the chicken pieces, peas and mushrooms and peppers. Serve hot in timbale cases with the sherry added at the last minute.

CHICKEN WITH NOODLES

4 tablespoons minced onion
1 ½ cups finely shredded
  cooked chicken
1 ¼ cups chicken stock
1 ½ tablespoons cornflour
3 tablespoons butter

1 cup button mushrooms
1 cup diced celery
¼ cup yoğurt
3 tablespoons water
Celery salt and mignonette
  pepper

Melt the butter in a deep stewpan and sauté the onions and mushrooms until very lightly browned. Add the shredded chicken, celery, stock and beaten yoğurt and simmer for 20 minutes. Add seasoning. Blend the cornflour and water, stir into neat mixture and stir until slightly thickened and clear. Serve this over 3 cups of noodles cooked in fast-boiling, salted water for 20 minutes, drained and rinsed in cold water.

This dish was given by an American who had lived in Istanbul so many years that cooking with yoğurt was as natural as breathing.

CHICKEN A LA PANDELI

1 4-lb chicken
¼ cup butter
6 tablespoons dry cider
  (or Sauternes)
2 ½ cups yoğurt
2 teaspoons paprika

Seasoned flour (½ cup flour,
  ½ teaspoon pepper, ½ teaspoon sweet marjoram, ½
  teaspoon paprika, 1 teaspoon
  garlic salt, combined well)

Clean and cut chicken into serving pieces and roll in the seasoned flour. Melt the butter in a large stewpan and brown chicken pieces. Add cider (or Sauternes), cover and cook in oven (325°) until tender (60 to 75 minutes), basting every 10 minutes. For the last 10 minutes remove the cover so that the crust will become crispy. Pour the yoğurt over and heat through. Sprinkle generously with paprika.

CHICKEN PRINTANIER

1 3-*lb spring chicken*   1 *cup chicken stock*
1 *large onion*   ½ *cup butter*
2 *cups yoğurt*   Salt *and pepper*

Cut chicken in serving pieces. Sauté onion in butter and when transparent add the pieces of chicken and fry until delicately browned. Add salt and pepper and stock. Cover and simmer until chicken is tender. When almost done add the yoğurt and heat through. Serve with buttered green peas.

CHICKEN WITH RED BURGUNDY

1 3-lb chicken
½ cup Cognac
½ cup flour
6 tablespoons butter
1 cup button onions
Enough Beaujolais to cover

1½ cups button mushrooms
¼ teaspoon paprika
1 bouquet garni (thyme,
  sage, chervil, parsley)
½ cup yoğurt
Salt and pepper

Cut the chicken in serving pieces. Pour over it the warmed Cognac, and ignite. Roll the chicken pieces in flour. Melt the butter in a deep stewpan and brown the chicken. Add the Beaujolais and the bouquet garni (which should be tied in a muslin bag) and cover and cook gently for 45 minutes. Sauté the onions until transparent, add mushrooms and cook the whole until tender. Remove from heat and arrange on a hot dish. Place the chicken in the centre, remove the bouquet garni from the wine sauce, strain the sauce, boil rapidly to reduce by half and pour over the chicken.

Just before serving, add the yoğurt, unbeaten, and sprinkle with paprika.

SALMI OF WILD DUCK

1 duck
½ cup Port
½ cup stock
2 tablespoons butter
½ cup skinned chestnuts

2 tablespoons flour
½ cup Cognac
½ cup yoğurt
½ teaspoon lemon juice
Salt and pepper

Roast the duck in a hot oven (450°) for 25–30 minutes, basting continuously. Remove from oven and keep warm.

Heat the butter and stir in the flour. Add Port and stock and cook until reduced by one-half. Remove from heat and add the beaten yoğurt, lemon juice and any blood and gravy left in the roasting dish. Stir well, heat again and reduce by one-third. Fillet the duck, pour the Cognac over and ignite. Arrange the pieces on a serving dish, surrounded by the chestnuts, and pour the strained sauce over. Serve at once.

SARAY DUCK

¼ cup butter
1 duck
3 tablespoons Madeira
1 cup white stock
1 cup yoğurt

½ cup button onions
½ cup black olives (pitted)
½ cup green olives (stuffed)
Salt and pepper

Melt the butter in a stewpan and brown the duck. Remove duck and sprinkle with Madeira. Keep hot. In a separate pan put the white stock and the yoğurt and stir well. Add the duck, salt and pepper and cook gently until tender.

Meanwhile, cook the onions in the butter which remains in the large stewpan and one minute before they are finished add the black olives. Dish up the duck on a hot platter, surrounded with the onions and olives and garnished with the stuffed green olives. Serve at once.

SUT KUZUSU (BABY LAMB)

3 lb sucking lamb   6 tablespoons white wine
4 small onions   1 cup yoğurt
2 tablespoons butter   Salt to taste
2 tablespoons minced fresh dill

Melt butter in a stewpan. Cut the lamb into pieces the size
of an egg. Add to the butter with the onions. Cover and
cook on a low heat for 2 or 3 minutes, shaking stewpan
continuously to avoid burning. Add the wine. Cover and
cook until meat is tender, basting every 15 minutes with
the wine. Add the minced dill and serve at once. Hand
small dishes of yoğurt separately.

LAMB EN GELEE

2 cups marrow-bone stock   4 tablespoons cold water
2 tablespoons gelatin   ¼ cup heavy cream
1 cup yoğurt   12 small tomatoes, skinned
24 radishes   and whole
Flowerlet of parsley   Salt and pepper
3½ cups cooked, sliced lamb

Stir the gelatin into the cold water and dissolve in the hot
marrow-bone stock. Stir well and cool until very slightly
thickened. Add the lamb seasoning, pour into an oiled dish
and chill until set. Unmould on serving plate. Beat the
yoğurt several times, combine with the cream and beat
again. Spoon this mixture round the edge of the serving

dish, garnish with radish flowers and tomatoes and set the parsley on top of the jellied mould.

LAMB KIDNEY YOGURT

6 *lamb kidneys*
1 *tablespoon lemon juice*
1 *teaspoon minced chives*

2 *tablespoons butter*
½ *cup yoğurt*
Celery salt and pepper

Wash the kidneys, remove the outer membrane and split through the centre lengthwise. Remove the fat and white tissue and soak in cold salted water for 15 minutes. Dry very carefully and brush with the butter (melted). Grill for 10–15 minutes, according to their size, turning once only. Season and sprinkle with lemon juice. Serve immediately with the unbeaten yoğurt spooned over them and garnished with chives.

BRAISED LAMB SHANKS

1 *lb lamb shanks*
2 *tablespoons good fat*
1 *cup bone stock*
1 *cup young carrots*

½ *cup yoğurt*
½ *cup sliced mushrooms*
½ *cup sliced onions*
Celery salt and pepper

Brown the shanks in a deep stewpan in hot fat, season and add the stock. Cover and simmer for 1 hour. Add the vegetables and well-beaten yoğurt, cover and cook for a further hour. Serve hot in its own juice.

LIVER ROULADE

6 *pieces of liver*   ¼ *cup yoğurt*
½ *cup toasted crumbs*   ¼ *cup bone stock*
1 *tablespoon chopped chives* 4 *tablespoons red wine*
½ *teaspoon sage*   ½ *teaspoon thyme*
6 *tablespoons butter*   **Garlic salt and pepper**

Combine the yoğurt, bread crumbs, seasoning and herbs and spread this over each piece of liver. Roll up and fasten with a small skewer. Brown in butter over medium heat, add bone stock and wine and simmer for 1½ hours. Serve hot.

PHEASANT AUX CERISES

1 *pheasant*   1 *cup cooked pitted cherries,*
3 *tablespoons white wine*   *semi-sweetened*
4 *tablespoons butter*   1 *tablespoon Marsala*
1 *onion, finely chopped*   **Salt and pepper**
1 *cup yoğurt*

Sprinkle the pheasant with the wine. Melt butter in a large stewpan and sauté the onion until transparent. Add the pheasant and cook for 30 minutes, shaking the pan frequently to prevent burning. Half-way through the cooking turn bird to brown on other side. Add the yoğurt, beaten, and cook another 15 minutes, basting frequently. Season. Serve on a hot dish, surrounded with the cherries which should have marinated for 2 hours in the Marsala.

With this dish it is advisable to aim for slight under-cooking rather than overcooking, as pheasant is very dry.

RISSOLES A LA TURQUE

1 lb finely minced lamb
2 tablespoons minced shallot
1 egg
⅛ teaspoon cinnamon
½ cup bread crumbs
½ cup beef stock

¼ cup yoğurt
½ cup red currant jelly
5 tablespoons butter
Mustard and cress
Garlic salt and pepper

Mix all the ingredients together, excepting the stock, butter and mustard and cress. Form into egg-shaped balls. Brown in the heated butter. Arrange in a baking dish, pour over them the stock, cover and bake at 350° for 1–1½ hours.

Serve hot with a garnishing of mustard and cress.

YOGURTLU PAÇA (SHEEP'S FEET)

6 *sheep's feet*	1 ½ *cups yoğurt*
10 *cups water*	½ *cup sheep's feet stock*
1 ½ *tablespoons lemon rind*	1 *clove garlic crushed in salt*
2 *cloves garlic*	1 *cucumber*
1 *tablespoon olive oil*	½ *tablespoon lemon juice*
Salt	3 *mint leaves*

Clean the sheep's feet and wash several times under running water. Put in a large stewpan with the water, lemon rind, garlic, olive oil and salt. Bring to boil and skim. Turn heat low and simmer until jellied, about 10 hours.

Whisk the yoğurt with the sheep's feet stock and the crushed garlic. Take the meat off the bones, chill and serve with the yoğurt mixture.

Hand separate dishes of finely sliced cucumber which has been sprinkled with lemon juice and garnished with a few mint leaves.

CREAMED SWEETBREADS

3 *lb sweetbreads*	1 *cup skinned tomatoes*
½ *cup minced lamb*	2 *tablespoons flour*
6 *tablespoons dry sherry*	2 *cups single cream*
1 *cup yoğurt*	½ *cup sliced mushrooms*
4 *tablespoons butter*	1 *tablespoon minced chives*
1 *teaspoon dry mustard*	*Salt and mignonette pepper*

Simmer the sweetbreads for 25 minutes in boiling, salted

water to which 1 tablespoon lemon juice has been added. Remove from heat, drain and plunge into cold water. Remove the membranes and when sweetbreads are quite cold cut into 1-inch pieces.

Melt the butter in a stewpan and sauté the mushrooms until light brown. Remove the mushrooms, leave aside and keep hot and put the minced lamb in the butter and fry for 5 minutes. Blend in the flour and remove the whole from the heat.

Beat the cream and the yoğurt together and add to meat mixture. Season and add the chives. Add sherry and bring to boil over a low heat – boil a bare minute, stirring all the time. Combine with the sweetbreads and the sautéed mushrooms and arrange in a buttered baking dish. Garnish with the tomatoes, left whole, and bake at 350° for 35 minutes. Serve hot.

SALÇALI DIL (TONGUE)

3 shallots
2 tablespoons butter
¼ cup milk
2 tablespoons flour
¼ cup cream
½ cup yoğurt

1 tablespoon tomato purée
2 tablespoons dry white wine
Salt and pepper
1 jar of lambs' tongue (stud
    with slivers of garlic)

Chop the shallots finely and cook in butter until soft. Add
the flour and stir well. Add very gradually the milk and
the cream. Beat the yoğurt for a few seconds, add to
mixture and allow to thicken, stirring constantly. Add the
tomato purée, wine and seasoning. Blend well together.
Simmer over hot water for 35 minutes (this sauce should
be of heavy cream consistency). Heat the lambs' tongues
and arrange on a serving dish. Cover with the sauce and
glaze under a hot grill for 6–8 minutes. Serve immediately.

MOUSSE OF TONGUE

1 tablespoon gelatin
½ cup hot beef stock
1 tablespoon dry mustard
1 tablespoon chopped green
    pepper
½ cup yoğurt
3 tablespoons cold water

2½ cups minced cooked
    tongue
1 tablespoon chopped
    pimento
½ cup heavy cream
Celery, salt, pepper,
    watercress

Put the gelatin in cold water, stir and dissolve in the hot

stock. Pour this over the tongue, add the mustard, peppers, seasonings. Whip the cream stiffly and fold into the tongue mixture. Pour into an oiled mould and chill until set. Unmould and garnish with unbeaten yoğurt and crisped watercress.

TURKEY A LA MANDALINA

1 *small turkey (cut at joints)*
9 *cups water*
¼ *cup butter*
2 *tablespoons chopped parsley*
1 *bay leaf*

1 *stalk of celery*
1 *large onion (quartered)*
2 *carrots*
3 *tangerines (skinned down to flesh and sliced)*

Put the turkey and all ingredients, excepting butter and tangerines, into a large stewpan and bring to boil. Skim. Turn down heat and simmer until bird is tender. Remove from the stock and drain. Fry in the butter until nicely browned and serve with the following sauce:

1 *tablespoon butter*
1 *tablespoon flour*
1 *cup warm yoğurt*
2 *tablespoons tangerine rind (grated)*

Pinch of ground peppercorn
3 *egg yolks*
Salt and pepper

Melt the butter in a pan, add flour and blend well. Add the yoğurt and simmer until thick. Add the tangerine rind, peppercorn and seasoning. Strain and add the beaten egg yolks. Heat through but do not boil as this will curdle the eggs.

Arrange the browned turkey on a serving dish, cover with the yoğurt mixture and garnish with slices of tangerine.

VEAL A LA BURSA

1 *lb veal steak*
2 *tablespoons minced onion*
¼ *cup yoğurt*
1 *cup cooked macaroni*
4 *tablespoons butter*
1 *teaspoon sweet marjoram*
¼ *cup sliced tomatoes*

¼ *cup sliced mushrooms*
¼ *cup diced celery*
2 *tablespoons dry cider*
1 *bay leaf*
Garlic salt
Pepper

Have the steak boned. Pound with a mallet until very thin, season with garlic salt, pepper and the bay leaf and leave for 4 hours. Cut into 1-inch cubes and fry in hot butter until brown. Remove the meat from pan and put in the tomatoes, onion, mushrooms and celery. Cook for 7 minutes. Beat the yoğurt and add to mixture, heat through but do not allow to boil.

Arrange the macaroni in a buttered baking dish, add the veal cubes and pour over the yoğurt mixture. Cover and cook for 30 minutes at 325°. Serve hot.

VEAL CUTLETS

1 *lb veal cutlets*
¼ *cup butter*
1 *onion, minced*
4 *teaspoons poppy seed*
¼ *cup dry white wine*

2 *cups yoğurt*
3 *slices lemon*
Garlic salt
Mignonette pepper

Cut the meat into 1-inch cubes, season with the salt and pepper and marinate in the wine for 4 hours. Remove and wipe carefully. Heat the butter in a stewpan and sauté the pieces of veal for 5 minutes, add the onion, lemon slices and poppy seed and sauté another 5 minutes, shaking the pan continuously. Remove the veal and keep hot.

Add the wine from the marinade, bring to boil and reduce by about one-fifth. Strain the sauce, pour into a baking dish, add the meat and beaten yoğurt and cover and cook at 350° for 45–50 minutes. Serve hot.

STUFFED VEAL FILLETS

2 lb boned veal steak
¼ cup yoğurt
6 hard-boiled eggs
1 tablespoon minced chives
¼ cup pineapple (fresh)
½ teaspoon rosemary
¼ teaspoon cinnamon

6 tablespoons butter
2 cups marrow-bone stock
2 cups whole skinned
   tomatoes
¼ cup toasted crumbs
Garlic salt
Pepper

Pound the veal thinly, season, add rosemary and leave
for 2 hours. Chop the eggs finely, mix with the chives,
cinnamon, pineapple (which should be cut very finely),
bread crumbs and beaten yoğurt. Combine well and spread
over the veal steak. Moisten with 1 tablespoon marrow-
bone stock. Roll up and tie securely with string. Heat the
butter in a deep stewpan and brown the veal. Pour the
stock over and simmer for about 2 hours in a slow oven –
300°.

Fifteen minutes before the cooking is finished add the
tomatoes. Serve hot.

VEAL WITH PAPRIKA

3 lb breast of veal
3 tablespoons butter
1 sliced onion
1 sprig rosemary

1 cup chicken stock
2 cups yoğurt
1 tablespoon paprika
Salt and pepper

Blanch veal by putting in hot water and bringing to boil.

Rinse under cold water. Melt the butter in a stewpan and brown the onions. Add the veal, rosemary and chicken stock and simmer for about 2 hours. Season with salt and pepper. Remove meat and arrange on a hot dish, pouring over it the stock remaining in stewpan. Smother with thick yoğurt and sprinkle with the paprika. Serve at once.

DANA KIZARTMASI (VEAL STEAK)

1 *large onion (chopped finely)*
12 *button mushrooms*
7 *tablespoons butter*
2 *lb veal steak*
3 *tablespoons sifted flour*
½ *cup heavy cream*
½ *cup yoğurt*
Salt and pepper

Sauté onion and mushrooms in 3 tablespoons of the butter until cooked. Cut the veal into 1-inch strips and flour and sauté in remaining butter in a separate pan. Shake frequently to prevent burning. When cooked, remove from pan and keep hot. Add a little flour and seasoning to the butter left in the pan and pour in the cream very gradually. Beat the yoğurt two or three times and add to the cream mixture little by little, stirring all the time until thickened. Stir in the cooked onion and mushrooms.

Arrange the veal on a hot dish and smother with the sauce. Serve at once.

EGG DISHES

✦✧✦✧✦✧✦✧✦✧✦✧✦✧✦✧✦✧✦✧✦✧✦✧✦✧✦

EGGS EN COCOTTE

6 *pieces of salami*	½ *cup grated Parmesan*
8 *tablespoons yoğurt*	*Flowerlets of parsley*
6 *eggs*	*Salt and pepper*

Butter individual casseroles and place a piece of salami in each. Break two eggs into each. Add 2 tablespoons of yoğurt to each dish but do not let it cover the yolks. Season with salt and pepper. Sprinkle the cheese over the yoğurt (again taking care not to let any fall on the yolks).

Place in 360° oven for 10 minutes or until yolks are set. Serve in own dish with flowerlets of warmed parsley decorating each yolk.

PALAS EGGS

3 *very large tomatoes* (*skinned*)	1 *tablespoon minced parsley*
6 *eggs*	1 *cup yoğurt dressing*
1 *cup minced cooked chicken breast*	30 *black olives*

Cut the tomatoes in half and remove the pulpy inside. Put a cold poached egg in each. Arrange in a circle on a flat serving dish and heap the chicken breast in the centre. Chill for one hour. Mask the whole with yoğurt dressing. Garnish with parsley and arrange the black olives around the edge. (For *Yoğurt Dressing*, see page 103.)

SHIRRED EGGS

6 eggs
1 lb finely minced beef
1 onion finely chopped

2 tablespoons butter
6 tablespoons yoğurt
Salt and pepper

Sauté the onion in butter until transparent. Add the meat, stir well and cook 10–15 minutes until meat is tender. Pour into a buttered baking dish and make deep hollows for the eggs. Dot with butter and break in the eggs. Season and put 1 tablespoon yoğurt on each egg. Bake at 375° until eggs are set – about 15–20 minutes. Serve hot.

STUFFED EGGS

6 hard-boiled eggs
1 tablespoon fresh yoğurt
2 teaspoons sherry
½ teaspoon olive oil
⅛ teaspoon pepper

1 cup cooked spinach
  (chopped)
⅛ teaspoon French mustard
1 cup yoğurt dressing
Salt to taste

Cut a slice from the pointed end of each egg and remove the yolks, taking care not to break or damage the whites. Sieve the yolks and put in a bowl with the yoğurt, sherry, olive oil, pepper and mustard. Mix well together and fill the whites tightly. Stand the eggs upright on a bed of spinach and just before serving add the yoğurt dressing (page 103).

EGGS WITH WHITE WINE

2 shallots (very finely chopped)
1 cup button mushrooms
½ cup dry white wine
1 teaspoon chopped tarragon
½ teaspoon chopped sorrel

½ cup yoğurt
1 cup stuffed green
  olives
6 hard-boiled eggs
Salt and pepper

Sauté the shallots until golden brown. Boil the mushrooms in a very little water and add the wine, herbs and seasoning. Boil fiercely for 3 minutes. Add the shallots and the yoğurt and stir well. Heat thoroughly but do not allow to boil again. Chop the eggs (which should be freshly boiled and still hot) and pour over them the wine sauce. Surround with the olives and serve at once.

OEUFS A LA PASHA

6 *eggs*
6 *tablespoons minced*
onion
1 *tablespoon butter*

2 *tablespoons grated*
Parmesan
½ *cup yoğurt*
1 *clove crushed garlic*

Cook the onions in butter until transparent. Remove from heat and break the eggs over them, sprinkle with the Parmesan and cook for about 10 minutes in 450° oven until eggs are set and a gratin has formed. Heat the yoğurt, stirring all the time, remove before it boils and add the crushed garlic. Pour over the eggs and serve immediately.

VEGETABLES

ASPARAGUS WITH YOGURT DRESSING

2 lb asparagus
4 hard-boiled eggs

4 teaspoons minced parsley
1 cup yoğurt dressing (p. 103)

Clean the asparagus by breaking off hard ends of stalks and removing any tough scales. Wash quickly and tie in bundles of 12. Stand upright in boiling salted water and cook for five minutes. Drain off this water and refill with freshly boiling water. Cook 20–30 minutes. Remove from pan and drain. Arrange on a serving dish, chop the eggs roughly and pile over. Pour over the whisked yoğurt dressing (cold) and sprinkle with the minced parsley.

AUBERGINES FARCIS

2 large aubergines
½ cup chopped spring onions
   (including green stems)
½ cup sliced mushrooms
1 cup yoğurt
3 tablespoons flour

½ cup buttered bread
   crumbs
¼ cup grated carrots
5 tablespoons butter
Salt and pepper

Cut a thick slice off the aubergines and cook in boiling, salted water for about 15 minutes. Remove the pulp from the shell (leave about ¼-inch thick).

Sauté the onions, mushrooms and carrots in the butter for 4 or 5 minutes. Blend in the flour and the yoğurt, stirring continuously until boiling. Add the aubergine pulp (cut up) and season. Do not boil again. Fill the aubergine shells, top with the buttered bread crumbs and bake for 25 minutes in 350° oven. Serve very hot.

AUBERGINES FRITES

3 *large aubergines*	2 *cloves of garlic*
2 *tomatoes*	1 ½ *cups olive oil*
2 *green peppers*	1 *teaspoon salt*
1 *cup yoğurt*	

Select the aubergines with great care; they should be very dark in colour (almost black) and unwrinkled. Cut off the stalk and peel the skin in sections, giving a striped effect. The stripes of skin should be narrower than the stripes which have been skinned. Cut in thick rounds. Sprinkle with salt and a little lemon juice and leave for 40 minutes so that the bitter juice of the vegetable is withdrawn. Wash well under running water, dry and fry in the olive oil which must be sizzling hot. Brown both sides and remove to a serving plate.

In the same oil fry the green peppers (washed, seeds removed and cut into pieces) and the sliced tomatoes for 2 or 3 minutes. Arrange them beside the fried aubergines and cool. Pour over them the beaten yoğurt in which the garlic has been macerated. Serve at once, as aubergine loses quality if it is not crisp.

AUBERGINES A L'ITALIENNE

2 *large aubergines*
1 *cup thinly sliced green pepper*
2 *cups cooked spaghetti*
2 *cups diced tomatoes*
½ *cup beef bouillon*

½ *cup grated Gruyère*
½ *cup toasted bread crumbs*
2 *tablespoons flour (sifted)*
½ *cup fresh yoğurt*
2 *tablespoons butter*
Salt and pepper

Put the spaghetti in a well-buttered baking dish, add the tomatoes and green peppers in layers and sprinkle each layer with a little seasoning and flour. Cover with the aubergines (cut lengthwise in quarters and well cleaned so that no bitterness remains). Beat the bouillon and yoğurt a few times and pour over. Sprinkle with the Gruyère and bread crumbs and dot with butter. Bake 55–70 minutes in 350° oven. Serve hot.

BEETS WITH YOGURT

2 *cups raw beets (grated coarsely)*
1 *cup fresh yoğurt*
1 *teaspoon coriander seeds*

Cook the shredded beets in boiling salted water for about

10–12 minutes. Drain and fork into a fluffy mass. Pour on the yoğurt (unheated) and sprinkle with the coriander seeds. Serve immediately.

BROAD BEANS

1 lb broad beans
½ cup olive oil
1 cup whole spring onions
  (fried in olive oil)
2 tablespoons minced dill
2 tablespoons chopped mint
1 teaspoon sugar

½ tablespoon lemon juice
2 cups water
1 cup yoğurt
1 clove crushed garlic
1 teaspoon chopped savory
1 tablespoon coarse salt
Salt and pepper

Cut tops and string sides of the beans and wash thoroughly. Cut into 1-inch-long strips and put in a bowl. Add the salt and lemon juice, combine well.

Arrange in a large stewpan a layer of beans, place over them the dill, mint, savory and spring onions. Top with the remaining beans. Add olive oil, sugar and hot water and cover with greaseproof paper. Cook 1½–2 hours, until beans are tender and water reduced to a tablespoon or less. Chill. Whisk the yoğurt, add the crushed garlic and pour over the beans. Serve very cold.

BRUSSELS SPROUTS

2 lb sprouts
½ teaspoon nutmeg
½ cup cut-up tomatoes
¼ cup shaved toasted
 almonds

¼ cup grated Parmesan
1 cup fresh yoğurt
2 teaspoons chopped chives
Salt and pepper

Remove any discoloured leaves from the sprouts, cut off hard core at bottom and make a nick in it with a sharp knife. Place, head downwards, in cold salted water for 20 minutes in order that insects may be withdrawn. Wash several times under running water. Drop into boiling salted water and cook about 15–20 minutes until tender. Remove from heat and drain thoroughly. Place in a buttered casserole, arrange the tomatoes and chives over them. Sprinkle with nutmeg and season with salt and pepper. Pour over the yoğurt (previously whisked). Sprinkle with the grated cheese and toasted almonds and bake for 15 minutes in a hot oven (350°) until nicely browned. Serve hot.

SERBIAN CARROTS

2 cups carrots (cleaned and
 sliced)
2 tablespoons butter
½ teaspoon sugar
⅛ teaspoon nutmeg

½ cup cream
½ cup yoğurt
1 egg yolk ·
Minced chives
Salt and pepper

Put the carrots into boiling salted water and boil about

15 minutes (depending upon size and age) or until tender.
Remove from heat and drain. Add the butter, sugar and
nutmeg and mix well.

Combine cream and yoğurt, whisk a few times and
add to carrot mixture. Beat the egg yolk and stir in. Stir
until slightly thickened. Sprinkle with the minced chives
and serve at once.

CARROTS A LA SULTANA

6 *carrots*
½ *cup flour*
¼ *cup thinned chicken stock*
1½ *cups olive oil*
1 *egg white*

1 *cup yoğurt*
1 *clove crushed garlic*
2 *teaspoons lemon juice*
Salt and pepper

Scrape and clean the carrots and cut into thin rounds.
Sprinkle with lemon juice. Put the flour and salt in a bowl
and by degrees add the thinned stock and 1 tablespoon
olive oil. Mix to a smooth batter and stir in the egg white,
stiffly beaten.

Put the rest of the olive oil in a pan and heat to smoking
point. Dip the carrot rounds in the batter and fry until
nicely browned. Add the crushed garlic to the yoğurt,
whisk a few times and pour over the carrots. Serve at once
with thinly sliced cucumber.

BRAISED CELERY

2 *cups celery cut in small*
    pieces
2 *sprigs parsley*
1 *teaspoon sweet marjoram*
1 *finely sliced onion*

½ *cup beef bouillon*
¼ *cup fresh yoğurt*
½ *cup buttered bread*
    crumbs
Salt and pepper

Put the celery, parsley, sweet marjoram and onion slices in a well-buttered baking dish. Combine the bouillon and the yoğurt by beating well and pour over the vegetables. Season. Sprinkle with the bread crumbs and bake at 360° for 30–35 minutes. Serve hot.

CELERY WITH WINE

2 *cups celery cut into*
    small pieces
1 *cup chicken stock*
1 *teaspoon castor sugar*
3 *tablespoons butter*

2 *tablespoons flour*
¼ *cup Madeira*
½ *cup yoğurt*
Salt and pepper

Put the celery in a stewpan and cover with the chicken stock. Add sugar and seasoning and cook 20–25 minutes. Heat the butter. Add flour and when well blended add the wine. Transfer to celery in stock and bring to boil, stirring continuously. Remove from heat and stir in the whisked yoğurt. Serve with young spring chicken.

CUCUMBERS WITH YOGURT DRESSING

3 *large cucumbers* 1 *teaspoon minced dill*
Boiling water to cover 1 *teaspoon chives*
¾ *cup yogurt dressing* 3 *hard-boiled eggs*
1 *clove of garlic (crushed)* 1 *teaspoon tarragon vinegar*
1 *teaspoon salt* *Few sprigs young mint*

Wash cucumbers and if young and tender do not peel. If, however, peeling is necessary, peel downwards in sections giving a striped effect (the skin of the cucumber being the narrowest stripe). Slice paper thin and cover with boiling water. Leave to stand for 10 minutes. Drain immediately and plunge slices into iced water. Drain again, dry and chill for 1 hour.

Mix the yogurt dressing (p. 103) with the salt, garlic, herbs and vinegar. Beat vigorously a few times and add the cucumber slices to this mixture. Chop the eggs coarsely and pile on top. Garnish with the young mint. Serve very cold.

CREAMED LEEKS

1 lb leeks
1 cup yoğurt
1 egg yolk
½ cup brown crumbs
1 tablespoon minced onion
⅓ cup butter

¼ cup heavy cream
¼ cup soft white cheese
1 tablespoon lemon juice
Boiling salted water
Garlic salt and cayenne

Trim off the roots of the leeks and discard the outer leaves. Cut into 2-inch pieces and cook for about 40 minutes in boiling, salted water to which the lemon juice has been added. Remove from heat, drain and plunge into iced water. Leave for 15 minutes and drain again.

Melt the butter in a pan and sauté the leeks for 2 minutes, adding the minced onion for the last minute. Arrange the vegetables in a baking dish, sprinkle with garlic salt and a little cayenne. Beat the yoğurt and add to the cream, stir well and pour over the leeks. Add brown crumbs, beat egg yolk and pour over and top with the white cheese which should have been creamed thoroughly. Cook in a moderate oven (350°) until the cheese is evenly browned. Serve hot.

FRIED BABY MARROWS

3 baby marrows
½ cup flour
½ teaspoon salt
¼ cup water
1½ cups olive oil
1 egg

¼ cup sliced cucumber
1 cup yoğurt
1 clove crushed garlic
1 tablespoon minced parsley
1 tablespoon lemon juice
Salt and pepper

Scrape and cut off the ends of the marrows. Cut into fairly thick slices and sprinkle with salt and lemon juice. Leave aside for 10 minutes. Put the flour and a little salt in a basin, add the water and 1 tablespoon olive oil, slowly. Mix into a smooth paste and add the beaten egg. Pour the rest of the oil into a stewpan and bring to smoking heat. Dip the marrow slices in the batter and fry until nicely browned.

Combine the yoğurt, garlic and cucumber slices, beat a few times and pour over marrows just before serving.

MUSHROOMS WITH PILAV

2 *cups pilav (cooked in beef stock)*
1½ *cups button mushrooms*
4 *tablespoons butter*
1 *cup yoğurt*

½ *teaspoon Bovril*
2 *tablespoons chopped parsley*
1 *large tomato*
Salt and pepper

Make a pilav by putting 1½ cups of beef stock, a little salt and 1 tablespoon butter into a stewpan and allowing to boil. Add 1 cup of washed rice, cover and boil for about 5 minutes. Turn heat to low, let simmer 10 minutes. Remove from direct heat and leave to stand for 30 minutes. Stir with a wooden spoon to separate the grains.

Cook mushrooms in butter for 10 minutes. Add the Bovril and stir well. Beat the yoğurt a few times and add to the mushrooms. Do not allow to boil. Season to taste. Arrange a border of pilav on a serving dish, pile the mushrooms in the centre, garnish with the parsley and a few thin slices of tomatoes. Serve hot.

OIGNONS FARCIS A LA MEHMET

6 *large onions*   ¼ *cup yoğurt*
½ *cup minced cooked veal*   2 *sprigs of parsley*
½ *cup buttered bread crumbs* Salt and pepper

Peel the onions and cook in boiling, salted water until fairly tender – about 15 minutes. Drain and cool. Cut thin slices from the root ends, hollow out the centres carefully, leaving a shell half an inch thick. Chop the centres very finely and combine with the veal, salt and pepper, yoğurt (beaten) and a little of the bread crumbs. Fill the onion shells firmly. Top with the rest of the buttered crumbs and bake for 1 hour at 350°. Serve hot, decorated with a flowerlet of parsley to each onion.

SAUTEED PARSNIPS

2 *lb parsnips*   3 *tablespoons minced parsley*
1 *cup yoğurt*   Salt and pepper
¼ *cup butter*

Clean and scrape the parsnips, cut in half lengthwise and remove the core if tough. Drop into boiling, salted water and cook 12–15 minutes. Remove from heat and drain.

Melt the butter in a pan, add the parsnips and sauté for 8 minutes. Arrange in a serving dish, pour yoğurt over them, garnish with the parsley and serve hot.

STUFFED GREEN PEPPERS

6 *large peppers*
1 *cup yoğurt*
2 *cups minced beef*
1 *onion chopped*

¾ *cup buttered bread crumbs*
½ *cup sliced mushrooms*
4 *tablespoons butter*
Salt and pepper

Cut a thin slice from the stem end of each pepper, keeping the stalk on. Wash well, removing the seeds and membranes. Put in a deep kettle of boiling, salted water, cover and parboil for 5 minutes. Remove from heat and drain. Allow to cool before stuffing, as this renders the shells less liable to break. Melt the butter in a stewpan and sauté the onions until transparent. Add the mushroom slices and cook for 5 minutes, shaking pan to prevent sticking or burning. Add the minced beef and cook for another 5 minutes, stirring frequently. Remove from fire and cool. Season. Put mixture in a bowl and combine with the bread crumbs and beaten yoğurt. If the mixture is too solid add a little more yoğurt, but it must not be of sloppy consistency. Fill the peppers very firmly. Replace the tops. Stand upright on a shallow baking dish in about ¾ inch of water and bake for 30 or 40 minutes at 350° oven. Serve hot.

GREEN PEPPERS WITH YOGURT

6 green peppers
1 cup yoğurt
2 cloves crushed garlic

6 tomatoes, halved
¼ cup olive oil
Salt and pepper

Wash the peppers, cut off the stem and clean the insides, removing seeds and membranes. Sauté the peppers for 5 minutes in the olive oil, remove from heat and cool. Peel off the thin outer skins, chop and arrange on a serving dish.

Beat the yoğurt well, add crushed garlic and salt. Pour this mixture over the peppers and serve very cold, with the tomatoes arranged round the edge of the dish.

POTATO BALLS

6 potatoes
1 tablespoon flour
2 tablespoons toasted bread
    crumbs
3 egg yolks
1 tablespoon butter
¼ teaspoon celery salt

1 tablespoon yoğurt
¼ tablespoon sweet
    marjoram
Dash of cayenne
Beaten egg yolk and bread
    crumbs for frying

Cook the cleaned, scraped potatoes in boiling water until tender. Drain and dry over the heat, shaking to prevent burning. Mash well with the butter and yoğurt (beat the yoğurt smooth first). When cooled a little add the beaten egg yolks, sweet marjoram, bread crumbs and flour. Season with the celery salt and cayenne pepper. Mix the whole

well and shape into small balls. Dip in the egg yolk and
bread crumb mixture and fry in deep fat until golden
brown.

STUFFED POTATOES

6 *large potatoes*	⅛ *teaspoon nutmeg*
¾ *cup yoğurt*	6 *tablespoons minced*
6 *tablespoons white cheese*	*cooked tongue*
3 *tablespoons minced chives*	*Salt and pepper*

Wash the potatoes, rub the skins of each with some good
fat and bake at 400° for about 1–1¼ hours. Cool slightly.

Scoop out the insides, taking care to keep the shell intact
and firm and mix the insides with beaten yoğurt, white
cheese, chives, nutmeg and tongue. Season to taste. Pile
the mixture into shells, dot each with butter and brown
quickly in a very hot oven. Serve hot.

POTATOES A LA TURQUE

3 *lb boiled potatoes*   1 *tablespoon butter*
2 *tablespoons cream*   2 *tablespoons minced chives*
2 *tablespoons yoğurt*   ⅛ *teaspoon nutmeg*
3 *egg yolks*   *Paprika*
3 *egg whites*   *Garlic salt*

Mash the potatoes (which should be freshly boiled) add butter, cream and well-beaten yoğurt and combine altogether. Add seasoning, chives, beaten egg yolks and, at the last, fold in the stiffly beaten egg whites. Sprinkle with nutmeg, pour into a buttered soufflé dish and bake at 350° for 25–30 minutes.

SPINACH WITH EGGS

1 *lb spinach*   3 *tablespoons butter*
1 *onion, chopped*   1 *clove crushed garlic*
½ *cup yoğurt*   *Salt and pepper*
6 *eggs*

Clean and wash the spinach several times under running water. Cover with boiling, salted water and boil for 5 minutes. Remove from heat, drain and press all water from the leaves.

Melt the butter in a pan and sauté the onion for about 3 minutes. Add the spinach and seasoning and continue cooking for 20 minutes. Remove from heat, make 'nests' for the eggs in this mixture, and slip in the eggs, one by one. Cover, return to heat and cook 5 minutes or until the eggs are nicely set.

Mix the yoğurt and the garlic, add a little salt and beat a few times. Spoon this over the eggs and spinach and serve at once.

TOMATOES SUPREME

6 *large tomatoes*
½ *cup minced cooked chicken breast*
1 *tablespoon heavy cream*
3 *tablespoons buttered crumbs*

2 *tablespoons spring onions, finely chopped*
¼ *cup yoğurt*
3 *hard-boiled eggs*
6 *black olives, pitted*
Celery salt and pepper

Cut a thin slice from the top of each tomato, scoop out the centres and discard the pips. Mix the chicken breast, spring onions, seasoning, tomato pulp and buttered crumbs together. Add the cream and unbeaten yoğurt, and combine all very well. Fill the tomato shells and set upright on a shallow baking dish filled to ½ inch with water. Bake for 30–40 minutes. Just before serving, garnish with hard-boiled eggs (two quarters allowed to each tomato) with a black olive between each piece of egg. Serve hot or cold.

STUFFED VINE LEAVES

1 lb minced beef
2 chopped onions
2 tablespoons chopped dill
3 cups beef bouillon
1 cup yoğurt
4 tablespoons butter

¼ cup rice
¼ cup tomato purée
1 lb vine leaves
1 clove crushed garlic
Salt and pepper

Clean and wash the vine leaves, drop into boiling, salted water and cook for 5 minutes. Remove from heat, drain well, pressing out all water, cut the leaves in half down the centre vein and cut again crosswise. Leave aside.

Melt the butter in a stewpan and sauté the onions until just beginning to brown. Stir in the tomato purée, add 1 cup of bouillon and bring to boil. Add the washed rice, turn heat to very low and cook until all liquid has been absorbed by the rice –about 10 minutes. Remove from heat and cool. Add the meat, dill and seasoning and mix well.

Put 1 teaspoon of this mixture on each vine leaf quarter and roll into envelope shape, tucking in the edges neatly. Arrange the stuffed leaves in a deep kettle in several layers, pour over them the remaining 2 cups bouillon and cook for 45–50 minutes over a medium heat.

Add the crushed garlic to the yoğurt and beat well. Garnish the vine leaves with this and serve at once.

If the vine leaves are small use them whole instead of dividing into quarters.

YOGURT FLORENTINE

2 lb spinach
¼ cup rice
2 onions, finely chopped
1 cup veal stock
3 tablespoons butter

½ cup minced veal
1 tablespoon tomato purée
1 cup yŏgurt
Garlic salt
Paprika

Clean the spinach and wash several times under running water, making sure that all grit is removed. Chop the leaves coarsely and drop into boiling, salted water. Boil 3 minutes, remove from heat and drain, pressing all water from the leaves.

Melt the butter in a stewpan and sauté the onions until transparent. Add the veal and cook for another 5 minutes. Remove from heat and add to the spinach. Mix in the rice, dissolve the tomato purée in bouillon and pour over the whole. Cover and cook for 30–35 minutes and serve with a thick garnishing of unbeaten yŏgurt.

This is a very popular hot-weather dish in the Near East.

SALADS

AUBERGINE SALAD

3 *aubergines*	2 *cups lemon jelly*
3 *tablespoons olive oil*	*(unsweetened)*
¼ *cup heavy cream*	4 *tablespoons minced parsley*
1 *cup yoğurt dressing*	*Salt and mignonette*
3 *tablespoons white wine*	*Pepper*

Put the unpeeled aubergines over a naked flame and cook, turning constantly, until the skins look blackened and begin to split. Remove from flame, clean away the burned skin and put the inside pulp into a bowl. Add the olive oil, by degrees, wine and seasoning and mash thoroughly with a silver fork. Chill and just before serving arrange on a platter, surrounded with a border of chopped lemon jelly. Garnish with finely cut onion rings which have been rolled in minced parsley.

Beat the yoğurt dressing and combine with the cream. Hand separately at table.

AVOCADO SALAD

3 *large avocados*
1 ½ *cups grapefruit sections*
24 *stuffed green olives*

1 *cup melon cubes*
½ *cup tangerine slices*
1 *cup yoğurt dressing*

Cut the avocados in half, lengthwise, and remove stone. Scoop out flesh, cut into cubes and sprinkle with salt. Toss all fruits together lightly, chill thoroughly and just before serving add the yoğurt dressing.

BEEF SALAD

1 *lb cold beef cut into slices*
2 *cups cold, diced potatoes*
1 *cucumber, sliced thinly*
2 *avocado pears*
¼ *cup black olives (pitted)*

2 *tablespoons dry sherry*
1 *pimento (cut into thin strips)*
1 *cup yoğurt dressing*

Arrange slices of beef on plates. Surround with the potatoes (which should have been tossed in a little of the yoğurt dressing) and arrange the cucumber and pimento strips to form an attractive pattern. Slice the avocados in half, remove stone and fill with the pitted olives which should have marinated in the sherry for 2 hours. Serve with yoğurt dressing.

RED CABBAGE SALAD

1 lb red cabbage   2 stalks of celery
1 cup seedless raisins   ½ cup soft white cheese
1 cup yoğurt dressing   4 tablespoons wine vinegar
¼ cup heavy cream   ½ cup pitted black olives

Parboil the cabbage for 3 minutes. Drain and cool. Sprinkle
with wine vinegar 3 hours before using. Shred the leaves
and arrange on a platter. Form the cheese into tiny balls
and arrange in a circle, topping each one with a black olive.
Cut the celery finely, mix with the raisins and put in the
centre. Beat the yoğurt dressing and add the cream. Combine thoroughly and pour over the salad just before serving.

CHEESE SALAD

2 cups grated cheese   2 tablespoons finely
6 hard-boiled eggs   chopped gherkins
1 teaspoon dry mustard   1 teaspoon poppy seed
1 teaspoon grated horseradish Asparagus tips
1 cup yoğurt dressing   Salt and pepper

Arrange the cheese on a bed of crisp cos lettuce. Slice the
eggs in half, remove yolk and put through a sieve. Mix with
the seasonings, moisten with a little dressing and fill the
egg whites. Pour over yoğurt dressing and decorate with
asparagus tips.

COS LETTUCE SALAD

2 *hearts of cos lettuce*   1 *cup yoğurt dressing*
3 *tablespoons chopped dill pickles*   ½ *cup red peppers*

Cut each heart into four and arrange on a platter. Slice the peppers very finely, add the dill pickles and season. Arrange with the lettuce hearts and pour the yoğurt dressing over. Serve well chilled.

CUCUMBER SALAD

1 *sliced cucumber*   3 *hard-boiled eggs*
1 *tablespoon minced chives*   1 ½ *cups yoğurt dressing*
1 *cup grated white cabbage*   ¼ *cup sliced pimento*

Arrange the cucumber slices on a bed of grated cabbage, which has been tossed in half a cup of dressing, quarter the eggs and surround and garnish with chives and sliced pimento. Serve well chilled with yoğurt dressing.

DOLMABAHÇE SALAD

1 *cup sliced red apples*
  (*skin left on*)
¼ *cup fresh walnuts*
  (*chopped*)
24 *stuffed green olives*
1 *cup asparagus tips*
1 *cup white cheese*

1 *cup yoğurt dressing*
1 *cup diced celery*
1 *cup heavy cream*
2 *tablespoons minced chives*
1 *cup cooked chopped*
  spinach (*cold*)

Mix the cheese and celery together and arrange on a bed of spinach. Add the apples, walnuts and asparagus tips in an attractive pattern and surround with the olives.

Combine the dressing and the cream, beat a few times and pour over the salad just before serving. Garnish with chives.

ORANGE SALAD

4 *large oranges*
8 *tablespoons caster sugar*
3 *tablespoons curaçao*

¼ *cup yoğurt*
¼ *cup heavy cream*

Skin the oranges down to the flesh and cut into very small pieces. Sprinkle with the curaçao and the caster-sugar, layer by layer, and leave for 6 hours.

Beat the yoğurt and the cream together and spoon over the salad.

◊-◊

ARTICHAUTS A LA TURQUE

3 *small artichokes*	½ *teaspoon coriander seeds*
1 *cup water*	1 *teaspoon thyme*
¼ *cup olive oil*	½ *cup yoğurt*
Juice of 1 *small lemon*	*Salt and pepper*

Clean and pare the artichokes and cut off the leaves. Put into hot water to which 1 teaspoon lemon juice has been added and parboil for 10 minutes. Drain, plunge into iced water and drain again. Put 1 cup of water in a stewpan and add the oil, lemon juice, coriander seeds, seasoning and thyme and bring to the boil. Add the parboiled artichokes and cook for 20–25 minutes. Remove the artichokes, drain and chill. Beat the yoğurt and add to liquor in the stewpan away from the heat. Cool and just before serving spoon this mixture over the artichokes.

CELERY BONNE MAMAN

4 stalks of young celery
3 russet apples, unpeeled
¼ cup heavy cream
¼ cup yoğurt

1 tablespoon parsley, finely
  chopped
Celery salt
Pepper

Mince the celery and apples together and add the seasoning.
Beat the yoğurt and stir into the cream carefully. Pour this
over the apples and celery. Garnish with chopped parsley
and serve in individual glass dishes.

CUCUMBER DILIMLERI

1 cucumber
½ cup cooked salmon
3 hard-boiled eggs

½ cup fresh yoğurt
1 tablespoon minced chives .
Salt and pepper

Pound the salmon and put through a coarse sieve, add
seasoning. Cut the peeled cucumber into thick slices,
plunge into boiling water and parboil for 2 minutes. Cool
in iced water, drain thoroughly and arrange in dishes.
Garnish with the salmon and quartered eggs. Beat the
yoğurt until frothy and pour over with a sprinkle of chives.

SALTED HERRINGS WITH YOGURT

3 *fillets of salted herrings*
6 *soft herring roes*
½ *tablespoon wine vinegar*
4 *tablespoons yoğurt*

½ *teaspoon each of: minced onion, chervil, chives and tarragon*

Soak the cleaned fillets for 1 hour, then arrange on a large hors d'œuvre dish.

Mash the roes with the vinegar, yoğurt and herbs and garnish the herrings. Serve very cold.

TOMATOES POLONAISE

6 *medium-sized tomatoes*
1 *teaspoon wine vinegar*
2 *teaspoons olive oil*
½ *cup yoğurt*
1 *cup minced cooked tunny*

½ *tablespoon minced onion*
½ *tablespoon chopped tarragon*
1 *tablespoon mayonnaise*
Salt and pepper

Mix the tunny, herbs and mayonnaise to a purée and heap in the centre of a large hors d'œuvre dish. Cut the tomatoes in thin slices and marinate in the vinegar, olive oil and seasoning for ½ hour. Arrange in a circle around the fish and garnish with unbeaten yoğurt spooned over.

SAVOURIES

◇◇◇◇◇◇◇◇◇◇◇◇◇◇◇◇◇◇◇◇◇◇◇◇◇

CHILBIR

6 *rounds toast (kept hot)*	6 *slices cooked tongue*
6 *eggs*	2 *tablespoons soft butter*
3 *tablespoons butter*	1 *teaspoon paprika*
1 *cup fresh yoğurt*	6 *teaspoons chopped*
Salt *and pepper*	*pickled dill*

Melt 3 tablespoons butter in a pan, break the eggs on a plate
and slip one by one into the hot butter. Season with salt
and pepper and cook 2 or 3 minutes until eggs are firm,
basting continuously with the hot butter. Remove eggs
from heat.

Arrange one slice of tongue on each round of toast, slip
an egg on each and with a cutter cut toast, tongue and egg
into a round. Place on a hot serving dish. Beat the yoğurt
(unheated) until creamy and pour over. Work the paprika
into the 2 tablespoons butter and spoon over the rounds.
Decorate each with a teaspoon of pickled dill. Serve at
once.

TORTE AU FROMAGE
(CHEESE TORTE)

1 ½ *cups soft white cheese*
¼ *cup button mushrooms*
   (sliced)
1 *teaspoon grated lemon rind*
2 *or* 3 *egg whites*
⅓ *cup toasted bread crumbs*

½ *cup fresh yoğurt*
½ *cup heavy cream*
Shaved toasted almonds
Salt and pepper
Paprika

Cream and soften the cheese, and combine with the mushrooms and lemon rind. Add seasoning. Beat the egg whites
until stiff and fold into the cheese mixture. Pour into a
deep mould (8″ × 3″) which has been oiled and well dusted
with the bread crumbs. Bake at 350° until firm and set –
about 40 minutes. Mix together the yoğurt and cream,
beating vigorously 3 or 4 times and spread over the torte.
Decorate with the almonds and bake for five more minutes
at 475°. Sprinkle with paprika and serve at once.

MACARONI TIMBALE

6 tomatoes (skinned)
½ cup red wine
2 cups broken macaroni
6 cups boiling salted water
1½ cups finely chopped
   cooked tongue
1½ cups grated Gruyère

2 tablespoons butter
5 egg yolks
½ teaspoon grated nutmeg
½ teaspoon cinnamon
5 egg whites
1½ cups thick yoğurt
Salt and pepper

Put the tomatoes and wine in a saucepan and boil until reduced to a purée – this will take an hour or so.

Drop the macaroni into fast-boiling water and cook 15–20 minutes (keep it fairly firm). Drain and rinse in cold water. Mix with the tongue, cheese, butter, beaten egg yolks, nutmeg and cinnamon. Season to taste. Whisk the egg whites until stiff and fold in.

Line a buttered baking dish with the tomato purée and pour over it the macaroni mixture. Bake for about 35–40 minutes at 425°. Serve with the yoğurt which should have been heated through and whisked a few times.

NOODLES ORIENTALE

1 lb finely minced beef
1 cup toasted bread crumbs
½ cup yoğurt
1 clove crushed garlic
¼ cup grated Gruyère
   cheese

2 eggs (well beaten)
1 teaspoon chopped olives
½ teaspoon sweet marjoram
½ cup finely chopped
   onions
Parsley

Combine all together and form into flattened balls. Fry
until brown. Now mix in 2 tablespoons flour. Add:

3 cups sliced tomatoes   2 tablespoons dry cider
¼ cup sliced pimentos   Salt and pepper
2 cups button mushrooms

and simmer 1¼ hours. Serve hot over hot, boiled noodles
and sprinkle with chopped parsley.

SULTAN'S FAVOURITE

6 eggs   1½ tablespoons minced parsley
6 tomatoes   ½ cup yoğurt
6 chicken livers   ¼ cup buttered bread crumbs
½ clove garlic   Salt and pepper
2 tablespoons Madeira

Cut tomatoes in half and put them in a stewpan, cut side
down, with a little hot olive oil. When half cooked turn
them over, sprinkle with buttered bread crumbs, a little
finely chopped garlic and minced parsley. Remove from
heat the moment they are cooked. Butter a flat baking dish
and break in the eggs. Dot with butter and season to taste.
Cook in 350° oven for about 10 minutes, now and then
basting the yolks with the hot butter.

Arrange on a hot platter surrounded by the tomatoes
and the chicken livers, which should have been sautéed in
the Madeira for a few minutes over a fierce flame. Whisk
the yoğurt a few times and pour around the dish. Serve
at once.

DESSERTS

SPICED APPLES WITH
PORT WINE

1 *lb cooking apples*	¼ *cup* Port
¼ *cup brown sugar*	6 *tablespoons butter*
1 *teaspoon cinnamon*	¼ *cup yoğurt*

Peel and slice the apples thickly. Cook them in hot butter, burning continuously until they are soft and pale brown. Add the sugar, cinnamon and port and cook for 5 minutes more. Remove the apples and arrange in serving glasses. Strain the sauce and pour over them. Spoon on thick yoğurt and serve. Sprinkle lightly with caster-sugar.

APRICOT MARGARETE

1 *lb apricots*	6 *egg whites*
6 *egg yolks*	½ *cup mirabelle or apricot*
2½ *cups water*	*brandy*
1½ *cups caster-sugar*	¼ *cup yoğurt*
6 *tablespoons soft butter*	¼ *cup heavy cream*

Put the water and whichever liqueur is being used in a saucepan with the stoned, halved apricots and cook until fruit is barely tender. Remove the fruit, add the sugar to the saucepan and by fast boiling reduce to 2 cups.

Arrange the apricots, dotted with butter, in a baking dish and bake at 350° for 15 minutes. Pour in the two cups of syrup and cook another 15 minutes. Remove from oven and cool a little. Beat the egg yolks until thick and add to apricots, fold in the stiffly beaten egg whites and bake at the same temperature for a further 15 minutes or until top is delicately browned.

Beat the yŏgurt and the cream together and pour over apricots at table.

BLACKBERRY DESSERT

¾ *cup yoğurt*
1 *teaspoon soda*
3 *cups fine white crumbs*
½ *cup soft butter*
½ *cup vanilla sugar*
1 *cup self-raising flour*
1 *teaspoon salt*
¼ *cup pralined almonds*

1 *cup crushed blackberries*
1 *cup whole blackberries*
3 *tablespoons Marsala*
2 *egg yolks*
2 *egg whites*
2 *tablespoons caster-sugar*
1 *cup whipped cream*

Beat the yoğurt well and pour it over the bread crumbs. Cream the butter and sugar until light and fluffy and beat in the egg yolks with the salt. Add to the yoğurt mixture and stir well. Sift the flour and soda and stir into the batter alternately with the crushed, sieved blackberries. Add 1 tablespoon Marsala. Whisk the egg whites until stiff and fold in.

Pour into an oiled two-pint tube mould and steam for 3–3¼ hours. Let cool a few minutes, unmould and fill the centre with the whole blackberries which should have marinated three hours in the rest of the Marsala and the 2 tablespoons caster-sugar. Top with whipped cream and slivers of pralined almonds.

See *Macaroon Charlotte* (page 90) for directions how to praline almonds.

BOREK

5 egg yolks
½ teaspoon salt
3 tablespoons caster-sugar
2 tablespoons cognac

5 tablespoons yoğurt
2½ cups self-raising flour
  (sifted)
¼ cup butter

Put the egg yolks in a bowl, add salt and beat until thick and lemon coloured. Add the sugar and cognac and continue beating. Mix in the yoğurt and the flour alternately and knead on a well-floured board until the dough 'blisters'. Cut in 3-inch strips, slit each in the centre and pull one end through the slit. Fry in hot butter until pale brown. Drain well on greaseproof paper and sprinkle with caster-sugar mixed with icing sugar.

HURMA ABDULLAH

¼ *cup boiling water*
1 *cup cut-up dessert dates*
    (stoned)
3 *tablespoons soft butter*
½ *cup brown sugar*
2 *eggs*
1 ½ *cups self-raising flour*

½ *cup yoğurt*
¼ *cup single cream*
¼ *cup cognac*
2 *teaspoons grated lemon rind*
1 *teaspoon soda*
1 *teaspoon salt*

Pour the boiling water over the dates, stir well and work in the butter. Beat the eggs until thick and lemon coloured, add the sugar and blend this into the date mixture.

Sift flour, soda and salt, add lemon rind and combine with the other ingredients. Whisk the yoğurt and mix with cream and stir into batter. Pour into an oiled mould and steam for about 2½ hours. Leave to rest a few minutes then unmould on a hot serving plate. Pour cognac over and ignite at table. (The cognac should be warmed before pouring over as this helps it to ignite quickly.)

LOKMA WITH YOGURT

1 *cup yoğurt*
¼ *cup single cream*
2 *cups self-raising flour*
2 *eggs*
1 *level teaspoon soda*
1 *cup butter*

2 ½ *cups caster-sugar*
½ *cup thin honey*
½ *tablespoon lemon juice*
3 *cups water*
¼ *cup heavy cream*

Put the water, sugar and lemon juice in a stewpan and bring to the boil slowly, taking care not to burn the sugar. Boil for 5 minutes to make a syrup.

Beat the yoğurt, cream and eggs together. Sift the flour and soda and add by degrees to the yoğurt mixture, stirring until well blended.

Melt the butter and when it is sizzling hot drop in the batter in teaspoonsful. Cook until deep brown then drop each spoonful into the syrup. Leave for 5 minutes then arrange on a serving dish. Serve cold, split in two and spread with honey. Whip the heavy cream and decorate.

MACAROON CHARLOTTE

1 cup powdered macaroons   9 egg whites
2 cups yoğurt   9 egg yolks
¼ cup Grenadine   1½ cups icing sugar
1½ cups dessert pears   Pinch of salt
   (cooked, halved)

Put the powdered macaroons in a bowl and pour over them the Grenadine. Heat the yoğurt slightly, pour over macaroons and rub through muslin. Beat the egg yolks until thick and lemon coloured, add sugar and salt (sifted), stir well and combine gradually with the maracoon mixture. Beat the egg whites until stiff and fold in lightly. Pour into an oiled pan, stand in a shallow tin of water and cook in moderate oven (325°) for about 35 minutes.

Let the mould rest three or four minutes before turning out. Unmould on a serving plate and surround the base with the halved, drained pears filled with Grenadine-flavoured whipped cream. Top with pralined almonds.

To praline almonds

Chop some almonds and brown evenly in the oven, sprinkling them frequently with icing sugar. The heat of the oven caramelises the almonds.

PINEAPPLE ROYALE

3 egg yolks
¼ cup caster-sugar
¼ cup self-raising flour
   (sifted)
¼ pulped pineapple

1 cup yoğurt
1 teaspoon soda
3 egg whites
¼ teaspoon salt

In a mixing bowl sift the flour, sugar, salt and soda. Beat the yolks until thick and lemon coloured and mix with the dry ingredients. Stir in pulped pineapple. Beat the yoğurt a few times and add to mixture, combining well. Whisk egg whites until stiff and fold in. Pour into 6 serving glasses, set in shallow pan of water and cook 50–60 minutes at 350° until firm. Serve hot decorated with whole pineapple cubes rolled in chopped pistachio nuts and sweetened whipped cream.

POMEGRANATES BEDIA

3 *large pomegranates* 2 ½ *cups caster-sugar*
3 *small pomegranates* 2 *cups water*
¼ *cup yoğurt* ½ *tablespoon lemon juice*
¼ *cup heavy cream* ¼ *cup pralined almonds, halved*
6 *tablespoons rosewater* ¼ *cup ratafia biscuits, crushed*

Put the sugar, water and lemon juice in a saucepan and bring to the boil slowly, stirring continuously until all the sugar is dissolved. Boil for 12–15 minutes until a thick syrup is formed but taking care not to let the sugar burn. Remove from heat. In a serving dish arrange the large pomegranates from which the seeds have been removed. Sprinkle with the rosewater. Remove the seeds from the small fruits, take out the pulp and mash with the crushed ratafias. Fill the large halves tightly with this mixture and pour over them the syrup. Chill. Beat the yoğurt and the cream together and spoon over the pomegranates. Decorate with the pralined almonds (page 90).

RAISIN SPICED TORTE

2 *eggs* 1 *cup yoğurt*
1 *tablespoon sifted self-raising* 1 *cup seeded raisins*
  flour 1 *teaspoon grated lemon*
½ *cup sugar* *rind*
1 ½ *teaspoons cinnamon* ¼ *teaspoon salt*
½ *teaspoon ground cloves*

Beat the eggs until light and fluffy. Mix the flour, sugar, spices, salt and lemon rind together and add to eggs. Beat yoğurt until thinned and fold into mixture with the raisins. Pour into pastry-lined flan case and bake at 350° for 50–60 minutes.

RUM SOUFFLE

½ cup thick yoğurt
¼ cup single cream
¼ cup self-raising flour
  (sifted)
¼ cup butter

4 egg whites
4 egg yolks
½ teaspoon cream of tartar
½ cup caster-sugar
2 tablespoons rum

Melt the butter and blend in the flour. Beat the yoğurt vigorously and add the cream. Combine well with the butter and flour and cook over a low heat, stirring continuously, until thick and creamy. Remove from heat. Beat the egg yolks until thick and lemon coloured, add the sugar and rum gradually and stir into yoğurt mixture. Put the egg whites in a bowl with the cream of tartar and whip until very stiff. Fold into the batter. Pour the whole into a 4-pint soufflé dish, set in a shallow pan of water and bake about 50 minutes in 325° oven until pale brown. Serve hot with rum-flavoured whipped cream.

SARAY SOUFFLE

9 egg whites
¾ teaspoon cream of tartar
6 tablespoons caster-sugar
3 tablespoons curaçao

4 tablespoons fresh orange pulp
¼ teaspoon salt

Beat the egg whites with the cream of tartar and salt until stiff enough to hold a peak. Add, little by little, the sugar and curaçao. Fold in gently the orange pulp and pour into an oiled tube mould (10-inch size). Set in a pan of water and bake about 1½ hours in 275° oven or until set. Turn out on hot serving dish and serve with the following sauce:

2 egg yolks
½ cup sifted icing sugar

2 tablespoons curaçao
¼ cup yoğurt

Beat the yolks until thick and lemon coloured, beat in the icing sugar and the curaçao. Fold in ¼ cup thick, very fresh yoğurt.

This delicate soufflé must be kept hot until it is served or it may fall.

YOGURT TATLISI

1 *cup yoğurt*
1 ½ *cups icing sugar*
2 ½ *cups self-raising flour*
2 *tablespoons melted butter*
4 *egg yolks*
½ *teaspoon soda*

3 *cups caster-sugar*
3 *cups water*
½ *tablespoon lemon juice*
4 *egg whites*
Whipped cream
Pralined almonds

Beat the yoğurt until creamy, stir in the icing sugar and butter. Beat egg yolks until thick and lemon coloured and stir into the yoğurt mixture.

Sift the flour and soda and add to the batter, combining well. Fold in the stiffly beaten egg whites and pour into an oiled 9-inch tin. Bake at 350° for about 1 hour.

Put the caster-sugar, water and lemon juice in a saucepan and bring slowly to boiling point, stirring all the time. Boil for 5 minutes. Remove the cooked pudding from the oven and pour the boiling syrup over it very slowly (do not remove pudding from tin during this process) until all the syrup is absorbed. Leave to rest for 1 hour then cut into triangle shapes (in the tin still) and serve cold with whipped cream topped with whole pralined almonds (page 90).

GATEAUX

$\diamond\!\!\!\!\diamond\diamond\!\!\!\!\diamond\diamond\!\!\!\!\diamond\diamond\!\!\!\!\diamond\diamond\!\!\!\!\diamond\diamond\!\!\!\!\diamond\diamond\!\!\!\!\diamond\diamond\!\!\!\!\diamond\diamond\!\!\!\!\diamond\diamond\!\!\!\!\diamond\diamond\!\!\!\!\diamond\diamond\!\!\!\!\diamond\diamond\!\!\!\!\diamond\diamond\!\!\!\!\diamond$

ARABIAN NIGHTS GATEAU

¼ *cup soft butter*	½ *teaspoon nutmeg*
¼ *cup vanilla sugar*	½ *teaspoon cinnamon*
3 *eggs*	1 *tablespoon cocoa*
1 *cup self-raising flour*	½ *cup yoğurt*
½ *teaspoon soda*	1 *teaspoon lemon juice*
¼ *teaspoon salt*	¼ *cup ground almonds*

Cream the butter and sugar until white and fluffy. Beat in the eggs (2 minutes' beating for eggs) and add salt. Sift all the dry ingredients *three* times, excepting the almonds, and stir in alternately with the beaten yoğurt and lemon juice. Fold in the ground almonds.

Pour into two 8-inch tins, well oiled, and bake at 350° until cooked when tested – about 40 minutes. Cool and fill with Arabian Nights Icing (page 105).

BALKANS PETITS GATEAUX

2 tablespoons soft butter
½ cup caster-sugar
1 cup yoğurt
2 eggs
1 ¾ cups self-raising flour
¾ teaspoon soda

½ teaspoon salt
½ teaspoon ground cloves
½ teaspoon cinnamon
¼ teaspoon nutmeg
½ tablespoon grated orange
    rind

Cream the butter and half of the sugar until light and fluffy. Beat in the yoğurt and the rest of the sugar very gradually. Add the eggs, well beaten with the salt, and stir well, sprinkling in the orange rind at the same time. Sift the flour, soda and spices *twice* and add to the batter, stirring only enough to combine. Two-thirds fill oiled cupcake moulds and bake at 375° for about 20 minutes or until a silver knife thrust into the cakes comes out clean.

BANANA GATEAU

¼ *cup caster-sugar*
½ *cup soft butter*
2 *eggs*
3 *tablespoons yoğurt*
1 ½ *cups bananas*

2 *cups self-raising flour*
½ *teaspoon soda*
¼ *teaspoon salt*
¼ *cup chopped almonds*
½ *tablespoon rosewater*

Cream the butter and sugar until very light and fluffy. Beat the eggs and salt together for 1 minute and beat into the butter and sugar mixture. Stir in the beaten yoğurt, rosewater and the bananas which should have been cut into very thin rounds. Sift the flour and soda *twice* and stir into the batter slowly. Fold in the almonds last of all.

Pour the mixture into an oiled tin, leave to rest for half an hour and bake at 350° until a silver knife thrust into the centre comes out clean. Cool, and sprinkle top with icing sugar.

CHOCOLATE GATEAU A LA TURQUE

6 *squares plain chocolate*
¼ *cup soft butter*
¼ *cup vanilla sugar*
4 *egg yolks*
1 ½ *cups self-raising flour*

¼ *cup yoğurt*
¼ *cup cognac*
4 *egg whites*
¼ *teaspoon soda*
¼ *teaspoon salt*

Melt the chocolate in a little hot water, stirring until thick. Cream the butter and sugar. Beat the egg yolks with the salt until thick and lemon coloured and stir into the creamed butter mixture. Add the melted chocolate slowly.

Sift the flour and soda *three* times and stir in alternately with the whisked yoğurt. Add cognac and fold in the stiffly beaten egg whites. Pour into an oiled 9-inch square tin and bake at 345° until cooked when tested, about 50 minutes. Cool on a wire rack, split and decorate top and inside with the following special icing:

1 ½ *cups sifted icing sugar*	¼ *cup soft butter*
4 *tablespoons melted unsweetened chocolate*	*Sufficient cognac to bring to spreading consistency*

Combine all together and use as required. The top should also be garnished with white and purple crystallised violets.

In Turkey this delicious cake is reserved for Bayrams (religious festivals).

CHOCOLATE WALNUT GATEAU

¼ *cup soft butter*
½ *cup brown sugar*
3 *eggs*
2 *tablespoons unsweetened chocolate (melted in a little hot water)*
1 ¾ *cups self-raising flour*

½ *cup yoğurt*
¾ *teaspoon soda*
½ *teaspoon salt*
½ *teaspoon vanilla*
¾ *cup coarsely chopped walnuts*

Cream the butter and sugar until light. Beat the eggs for 1 minute, add the salt and stir into the creamed butter. Add the melted chocolate.

Sift the flour and soda and beat in alternately with the beaten yoğurt. Add vanilla.

Fold in the walnuts and pour into an oiled 9-inch square tin and cook at 350° until test shows cake is cooked – about 45 minutes. Cool, split in half and fill with rich chocolate filling made with melted chocolate, icing sugar and heavy cream combined well.

GATEAU MUAZZEZ

⅓ cup melted butter
3 eggs
¾ teaspoon soda
¾ cup yoğurt
⅛ cup cooked chopped prunes
¼ cup ground walnuts
¼ cup caster-sugar

1 ¾ cups self-raising flour
¼ teaspoon salt
⅛ cup cooked and finely chopped figs, drained of all juice
¼ cup seedless raisins cut into small pieces

Beat the eggs with the salt for 2 minutes, then beat in the sugar. Add the melted butter slowly and combine well. Sift the flour and the soda *twice* and blend in alternately with the whisked yoğurt. Fold in very carefully the cut-up fruits and the ground walnuts. Pour into two 8-inch oiled tins and bake until test shows cakes to be cooked – about 40 minutes. Cool and fill with sweetened whipped cream. Pipe rosettes of the whipped cream on top and decorate with crystallised rose-leaves.

◇◇◇◇◇◇◇◇◇◇◇◇◇◇◇◇◇◇◇◇◇◇◇◇◇◇◇

CACIK

2 *cups yoğurt*	2 *tablespoons wine vinegar*
¼ *cup water*	2 *tablespoons olive oil*
1 *large cucumber*	*Salt to taste*
2 *cloves garlic*	

Peel cucumber and chop finely. Add salt and leave aside
for 10 minutes. Beat the yoğurt with the water, crush the
garlic and add. Stir in the chopped cucumber and spoon
on the vinegar and olive oil.

This is a very refreshing summer sauce. Served with
meats or pilav dishes.

HORSERADISH SAUCE

½ *cup grated horseradish*	2 *tablespoons tarragon vinegar*
1 *cup yoğurt*	½ *teaspoon caster-sugar*
1 *tablespoon flour*	1 *teaspoon salt*
(*sifted*)	*Dash of cayenne*
1 *tablespoon butter*	

Melt the butter in a double boiler, add horseradish, yoğurt
and flour and stir constantly to avoid any lumps. Bring to

boil and cook until thick and creamy. Add the vinegar, salt,
sugar and cayenne. Stir well and serve cold.

YOGURT DRESSING

1 ½ *tablespoons sifted flour*	¼ *cup tarragon vinegar*
½ *teaspoon sugar*	2 *egg yolks*
½ *teaspoon salt*	½ *cup olive oil*
½ *teaspoon dry mustard*	¼ *cup yoğurt*
¾ *cup water*	2 *tablespoons minced chives*

Put all ingredients in a saucepan, excepting yolks, olive oil,
yoğurt and herbs, stirring all the time, and cook over a low
heat until the sauce thickens. Boil for 1 minute and remove
from heat. Beat in the egg yolks. Continue beating, adding
very gradually the olive oil. Chill thoroughly and 1 hour
before serving add the yoğurt and chives. Beat well for
half a minute.

YOGURT FRUIT DRESSING

1 *cup yoğurt*	1 *tablespoon pineapple juice*
2 *tablespoons thin honey*	1 *teaspoon grated lemon rind*
½ *teaspoon lemon juice*	⅛ *teaspoon salt*

Beat the yoğurt until frothy and add the other ingredients.
Mix well and serve with fresh fruit salads.

YOGURT HERB DRESSING

1 *cup yoğurt*
¼ *cup chopped celery leaves*
1 *teaspoon chopped parsley*
1 *tablespoon chopped chives*
1 *tablespoon lemon juice*
1 *tablespoon grated horseradish*
½ *teaspoon paprika*
½ *teaspoon garlic salt*

Beat the yoğurt until frothy and add the other ingredients. Serve with fish dishes.

YOGURT SAUCE

2 *egg yolks*
¾ *cup fresh yoğurt*
½ *tablespoon lemon juice*
½ *tablespoon minced parsley*
½ *tablespoon finely chopped dill*
Salt and paprika

Beat the egg yolks, add the yoğurt and lemon juice and heat in double boiler until thick and smooth. Season with the salt and paprika, add the herbs and combine well. Serve with vegetable dishes.

ICINGS AND FILLINGS

❖❖❖❖❖❖❖❖❖❖❖❖❖❖❖❖❖❖❖❖❖❖❖❖❖❖

ARABIAN NIGHTS ICING

3 tablespoons soft unsalted
   butter
1 large egg yolk
2½ cups sifted icing sugar

1 tablespoon very strong
   coffee (hot)
½ tablespoon cocoa

Cream the butter and add the egg yolk, beat a few times.
Add sugar and cocoa gradually (the cocoa should have
been sifted with sugar) and last of all mix in the hot coffee.
Beat the yoğurt and combine until a smooth, spreading
consistency is obtained. Use as a filling or top frosting with
Arabian Nights cake (page 96).

MARASCHINO ICING

2¼ cups sifted icing sugar
2 tablespoons beaten yoğurt

2 tablespoons soft unsalted
   butter

2 tablespoons Maraschino

Blend altogether well and use for fillings or toppings.
Decorate with whole glacé cherries.

YOGURT CREAM FILLING

3 *tablespoons soft unsalted
  butter*
1 ½ *cups icing sugar*
2 *tablespoons fresh yoğurt*

1 *tablespoon heavy cream*
Pinch of salt
Few drops of vanilla

Cream the butter and add the sifted sugar gradually. Mix until smooth and properly blended. Add the cream and the salt and beat well. Add yoğurt and vanilla and beat again. Use for layer cake filling or decoration.

AYRAN

HOW TO MAKE AYRAN

2 *cups yoğurt*
½ *teaspoon salt*

1 *cup iced water*
Mint leaves

Beat the yoğurt until frothy, about 5 minutes. Add the salt and iced water and beat for another 2 minutes. Serve in tall glasses garnished with sprays of mint leaves.

INDEX